# RAISING
# CONFIDENT
# KIDS

# RAISING CONFIDENT KIDS

NADIM SAAD

First published by
Best of Parenting Publishing
242 Acklam Road, London, W10 5JJ, United Kingdom
www.bestofparenting.com

ISBN: 978-0-9931743-5-3

Cover Design and typesetting by Danijela Mijailović

Set in Minion Pro

Raising Confident Kids is written and published as an information resource and guide intended to educate the reader of what they can do to improve their parenting. Although every effort has been made to ensure the contents of this book are accurate, the in-formation provided is not meant to take the place of expert psychiatric advice from professionals. The author cannot be held responsible for any loss or damage suffered as a result of complete reliance on any of this book's contents or any errors or omissions herein.

# Contents

# Introduction

*"If parents want to give their children a gift, the best thing they can do is to teach them to love challenges, be intrigued by mistakes, enjoy effort, and keep on learning. That way, their children don't have to be slaves of praise. They will have a lifelong way to build and repair their own confidence..."*

**Carol S. Dweck - Professor at Stanford and Author of 'Mindset - The psychology of success'**

As parents, we all want to raise confident children who thrive. Yet for decades, parenting experts had it all wrong as they believed that confidence and self-esteem could be boosted by praising children with words such as 'You're smart' and 'Well done'. Extensive research done in the last decade shows that this can be detrimental and even damaging to children. Other research shows that self-esteem comes from the 'inside out' rather than from the words we choose to use when communicating with our children.

So if praising children with 'Good boy' or 'You're so clever' doesn't work, does this mean that we cannot influence our children's confidence and self-esteem at all? Well thankfully, the latest parenting research shows that there are effective ways to boost children's self-esteem and confidence and maximize their chances of long-term success. So this book's objective is to equip you with tools that will help you develop your children's confidence and self-esteem in order to make them wiser, more resilient and better able to cope with life's challenges.

Self-esteem and confidence are very closely related, and we need a healthy level of both in order to be able to cope with the challenges of life and all of its inevitable 'ups and downs'. Self-esteem is our cognitive and, above all, emotional appraisal of our own worth. More than that, it is the matrix through which we think, feel, and act, and reflects and determines our relation to ourselves, to others, and to the world.[1]

While self-esteem is quite an abstract concept because it is essentially a reflection of our inner self, confidence is related to action and the way in which we relate or engage with the external world around us. Confidence can be learned and developed; we can become better at something through practice and repetition. But a high level of confidence alone might not be enough for a person to thrive and particularly to be happy because a person can be confident in one area of their lives and completely unconfident in another. Indeed, it is possible for a person to have high self-confidence and low self-esteem - and a lack of self-esteem can be particularly damaging. Because, although a person with a high level of confidence is more likely to seize opportunities and take on new challenges, even if the outcome is successful, if they lack self-esteem they may not feel good about - or reward themselves - for their achievements.

A high level of confidence and self-esteem are both key to being successful in all aspects of life, both personal and professional. They play a massive role in how we think and feel about ourselves and our behaviour tends to reflect those thoughts and feelings, whether they happen to be positive or negative.

We start to develop confidence and self-esteem during infancy and this is greatly influenced by our parents' interactions with us. For a child to develop a healthy level of both, they need to feel that they are loved by those who are closest to them and have a strong belief in their own capabilities. This allows children to approach new challenges with confidence and better equips them to be able to cope with hurt, disappointment and frustration.

As one would expect, research shows that children with high levels of confidence and self-esteem tend to be more independent and are more likely to perform well at school and grow to become happy and successful adults. They also tend to be 'smarter', not because they naturally have a higher IQ - which is only one measure of intelligence - than their peers, but because they will have developed their EQ (Emotional Intelligence) and they have assimilated that their intelligence and abilities can be developed and improved over time. Indeed, other research[2] shows that approximately only 25% of achievement is due to innate intelligence or IQ while the other 75% is attributed to psychological skills (such as persistence, grit, and resilience), which is what this book will focus on.

While self-esteem levels do tend to fluctuate slightly at different stages of a child's development, it's important to be able to recognize the signs if your child is lacking confidence in his/her abilities. This could be as a result of some external influence that's outside of your control, or it could be due to a negative experience that your child has had. Whatever the underlying cause may be, children with low self-esteem typically lack confidence in their abilities and have a tendency to 'talk themselves out' of trying new things. This is because they are often so afraid of making mistakes that they tend to avoid taking on new challenges for fear of not being 'good enough'.

One of the stories that really struck us as a perfect example of the potential to develop a growth mindset at any age is that of Dominic O'Brien, eight time World Memory Champion.[3] O'Brien overcame criticism and personal challenges with self-belief, practice and sustained effort and hard work and went on to achieve one of the most impressive feats of mental agility that the world has ever seen. This story is an amazing example of a growth mindset, particularly because O'Brien only managed to overturn his challenges in his thirties. It is a great one to share with kids to help illustrate the fact that intelligence is not fixed and that we can change our mindset at any age even if we have encountered difficulties in life.

As a child, Dominic O'Brien was diagnosed with dyslexia and was told by a teacher at a young age that he 'would not amount to much in life'. Unsurprisingly, this had a profoundly negative impact upon his self-esteem, and as a result he grew increasingly stressed and reluctant to go to school each day. This wasn't helped by the fact that his teachers were so frustrated with his apathy and apparent lack of effort that they would literally sometimes try to shake him out of his educational stupor.

O'Brien describes how at that time, he felt as though his brain was like a muscle, but that it was in a permanent state of relaxation and in very real danger of atrophy. His situation and feelings towards school didn't improve over the following years, in fact if anything they got worse. The day he left school (at the earliest opportunity) he said it felt at the time, like one of the happiest days of his life. Fast forward to 15 years later and O'Brien went on to perform such an impressive feat of mental agility that it led to him being crowned 'World Memory Champion', on no less than eight separate occasions.

O'Brien's 'memory journey' as he describes it all began in 1987 when he was 30 years old and watching TV. The program featured Creighton Carvello, an accomplished memory man of the time, remembering an arbitrary sequence of 52 playing cards. O'Brien was fascinated - he was so impressed and curious to know how Carvello had achieved this remarkable feat, that he sat down with a deck of cards and decided that the best way of working out whether it was possible was by attempting it himself.

With practice, dedication and sustained hard work, he did learn how to memorize that deck of playing cards, and this led to the realization that if he set his mind to something, he could achieve absolutely anything. He gained self-esteem and a level of confidence that he'd never had before, and he describes feeling as though a whole new world of opportunity opened up before him.

O'Brien discovered that there are no limits to where a growth mindset can take you, and his story demonstrates that intelligence isn't something that we are born with and isn't 'set in stone' as many people believe. It proves that with effort, patience and hard work, even the seemingly most unlikely of people can go on to achieve the most amazing of things.

Thankfully, there are steps that you can take at any age to develop your child's mindset and to unleash their potential. This starts by becoming more aware of the impact your words and actions have upon the way your child feels about themselves, and that's exactly what this book is designed to help you do. It will show you how to avoid some of the most common 'parenting traps' such as over-praising and motivating through rewards, and provide you with effective alternatives that will help you develop and nurture your child's confidence and self-esteem and maximize their chances of growing to become happy, successful and resilient adults.

# CHAPTER 1

## Typical Parenting Mistakes that Affect Children's Self-Esteem

*"You can't let praise or criticism get to you.*
*It's a weakness to get caught up in either one"*
**John Wooden**

Every parent wants to boost their children's self-esteem and confidence. However, the latest research shows that some of the things that parents do with the best of intentions can actually be detrimental to a child's self-esteem, particularly because our actions can make children doubt our sincerity and cause them to become afraid of failure.

Here are the 6 most common mistakes that parents make, usually due to a lack of awareness of their consequences:

## 1. Using evaluative praise

One of the keys to developing a child's self-esteem is to make them feel good about themselves and many parents think that the best way of doing this is by ensuring that children receive lots of praise and encouragement. And whilst it is true that some forms of praise and positive comments made to our children are likely to motivate them, research shows that certain types of praise can actually do more harm than good.

Indeed, research suggests that using evaluative praise with statements such as "You're smart" or "You're good at this" can create a fear of failure, because children become afraid to do anything that could expose their 'flaws' and call into question their 'talent'.[4] And yet such praise is commonly used by parents because it used to be advised by parenting experts in the 'self-esteem building culture' of the last couple of decades. Using such evaluative phrases focuses on our children's 'innate' talents rather than their ability to develop new skills, and we run the risk of boxing them into adopting a certain identity. Because if a child identifies as being 'smart' or 'good', they may feel as though they have to live up to that perception all the time, and this pressure can lead to children becoming afraid of failure.

Such pressure results in children becoming less likely to try new things or taking risks for fear of not getting it 'right' and so they end up missing out on essential opportunities to develop their confidence and sense of self. They are also likely to start disregarding their parents' appreciation of them because they grow to become cynical of this praise and may doubt its sincerity.

Rather than making children feel better about themselves, evaluative praise often has the opposite effect, in that it can cause them to focus on their weaknesses. For example, if we tell our child that they are an excellent reader, their reaction might be, "How can I be an excellent reader? It took me twice as long to finish the book than all the other kids in my class". It can also lead to feelings of immediate denial and disbelief: "I don't know why they're praising my drawing when the one I did yesterday was so much better - they're just saying this to make me feel good." Or in some cases, it can even be experienced as manipulation: "I haven't done anything to deserve the praise they're giving me, they must only be saying it because they want something from me".

Even though we may use it with the best of intentions, evaluative praise puts too much pressure on children to live up to our idealized perception of their ability and 'talents' and often serves only to make children feel uncomfortable. Indeed, many parents find that the more praise they try to give as their child grows up, the quicker their child is to reject it!

That's not to say that we should avoid praising our children, in fact quite the opposite is true. The key is to praise in a more effective way in order to develop a growth mindset, as we will see in the following chapters.

## 2. Focusing on the outcome

If we tend to focus on the outcomes by praising them with statements such as: "I'm so proud of you for getting 100% in your school test", we can inadvertently overlook the effort that our children have put in on the occasions when they don't excel or aren't successful in an exam or activity. As we will see in the following chapters, the effort that they put into something and the potential mistakes that they make when they don't get it 'right' are usually more valuable experiences for developing self-esteem than the outcome itself.

Also, if we only praise our children if they achieve a good outcome, then we run the risk of making them feel as though they have to 'win' or be successful every time, and if they don't achieve it then they are somehow failing. For some children, this feeling can make them afraid to take on new challenges - this fear is often driven by the worry that they will disappoint us if they fail to excel, so they start to avoid situations and challenges that may expose them as lacking in ability.

It can also cause children to think that if they don't reach the desired outcome (scoring highly in a test, winning a football match etc.) then they won't receive their parent's praise. And for many children, this apparent withholding of praise can feel like a criticism.

## 3. Criticising and comparing to others

There is nothing more demotivating for a child than receiving a constant 'diet' of corrective feedback or 'constructive criticism'.[5] This can make them feel singled out and as if they're being shamed for aspects of their personality or behavior.

And yet, it is quite easy to find ourselves as parents in 'error detection' or 'fault finding' mode, particularly when we feel that our child is being lazy and is not putting enough effort into a task or activity. This is particularly true when it comes to exams and grades. It is tempting to look at an exam and point out all the mistakes and this is particularly demotivating for children.

When we focus on highlighting what the child has done well instead, it boosts their confidence and makes them believe that they are capable and that they will be able to improve. When we do need to provide feedback, it's important that we try to do it in a way that will not affect their confidence. (See Chapter 3 for more ideas on how to do this.) It is also essential that we avoid comparing them to a better-behaved sibling or school friend as this is also demotivating, and it could send children the message that they have innate flaws and therefore have little to no capacity to change.

## 4. Overpraising and going overboard

Giving children constant praise for even the slightest of achievements may seem like a good way of increasing their confidence, helping them to become more competent and improving behavior. This type of constant 'positive reinforcement' is actually still advocated by a lot of parenting experts nowadays. However, research shows that praising children indiscriminately means that our praise is likely to become meaningless to them and loses its power to influence over time.[6]

By being praised for everything they do, children are likely to become 'praise junkies' and to be overly influenced by what other people think of them as they are so used to being evaluated. This also makes it more likely that they will become 'people-pleasers' as adults who seek constant validation from other people. As a result, they may find themselves frequently being either 'made' or 'broken' by someone else's opinion of them.

Similarly, if we become over-excited when praising children for the slightest of achievements, this can make them doubt our sincerity. In other words, if we go too 'over the top', we may find that in the long-term our children become cynical of our praise and start to doubt the sincerity of the appreciation we have for them. Children are very good at sensing when we are not being authentic in our interactions with them, so if we do this too often we may find that it starts to negatively impact upon the trust and connection we have with them.

This is especially true of older children; while young children will tend to accept what we say without question, teenagers are usually more aware of the possible motives behind our words and actions. With maturity comes a certain level of cynicism as well as the ability to question, so keep this in mind when praising older child

## 5. Using reward systems & sticker charts

Rewards and sticker chart systems have become hugely popular over recent years; parents use them as a means to encourage good behavior from their children and help them develop a positive attitude towards daily tasks and household chores.

Whilst such systems can certainly be effective in the short-term, the reward chart system teaches kids that the only point in being well-behaved is that they will be rewarded for it. Indeed, research shows that the external motivation provided by the reward becomes stronger than the internal motivation of simply behaving the way they should.[7] This means that if we constantly reward our children for something now, we are effectively reducing the chance for them to repeat that behavior again unless they are cajoled with more rewards.

This can be difficult for some parents to accept, as rewards and sticker charts often tend to produce quick and impressive results. However, the change in behavior is unlikely to last because such reward systems only focus on increasing the external motivation of the child, rather than having any real effect on their beliefs or attitude. This is because rewards don't encourage children to think about or take responsibility for their behavior, don't help to teach them 'right from wrong' and nor do they have any influence upon their moral development.

They are essentially a way of 'bribing' our children to do as we ask and once we remove the reward, the good behavior disappears with it. In the long-term, parents are very likely to find that their children come to expect greater and greater rewards, so that by the time they become teenagers, they may refuse to comply with any of our requests without some form of reward such as a financial incentive.

## 6. Focusing on your feelings rather than your children's

When our child does something we're proud of, it's only natural to want to tell them so, for example, "I'm so proud of you!" or "You've really impressed me" are two of the most common phrases that parents find themselves saying. Although such phrases are innocuous and well-meaning, these are still evaluations of a child's actions and it puts the focus on what we think about the situation without leaving room for the child to make their own self-evaluation.

Children could also interpret such statements as meaning that it's more important to impress their parents and make us proud of them than it is to simply take part in an activity for the sake of learning, growing and developing as a person.

## You do most of the above? Do not despair!

If you're used to making some or all of the mistakes listed above, which are very common, do not despair. Because this book's objective is to equip you with more effective ways of praising that will help to raise your child's level of self-esteem and maximize their chances of growing to become confident and independent adults.

# CHAPTER 2

# Fixed and Growth Mindset

*"A pessimist sees the difficulty in every opportunity, an optimist sees the opportunity in every difficulty"*
**Winston Churchill**

Recent research has made significant discoveries in the understanding of what makes children want to take on challenges and why they can become afraid of mistakes. And consequently, the effect this can have on their confidence, self-esteem and level of resilience.

For ten years, psychologist Carol Dweck[8] and her team at Columbia and Stanford examined a group of primary school children and focused on how they responded to praise. She discovered that children tend toward one of two mindsets. The first is a fixed mindset, when a child believes that his or her intelligence is 'set in stone' and will therefore only choose tasks that they deem appropriate to this level of intelligence, lest they risk failure. The second, healthier mindset is the growth mindset belonging to the child who is happy to take on new challenges because they see them as opportunities for growth and new experience, even if this involves making mistakes.

Dweck discovered that a child's experience of praise had a direct influence over which of these mindsets children were more likely to adopt. The first group of 'failure-fearing' children were generally used to being praised for their intelligence with words such as 'you're smart/clever', whereas the second group possessed more of a 'try and try again' attitude and were more familiar with being praised for their effort rather than the outcome.

As Carol Dweck explains, "emphasizing effort gives a child a variable that they can control. They come to see themselves as in control of their success. emphasizing natural intelligence takes it out of the child's control, and it provides no good recipe for responding to a failure."

## The implications of a fixed mindset in children

People with a fixed mindset believe that their basic level of intelligence, skill and ability is 'fixed' from birth and therefore can't be developed or improved over time. So when a child has a fixed mindset, this can affect everything from their attitude to learning and education right through to their willingness to take on new challenges or try new things. Children are unlikely to take part in an activity, whether it be a sport or something educational, if they don't believe that they can develop their ability and get better at it over time. They are far more likely to stick with the things that they are good at in the belief that that is where their 'natural' abilities lie. Because if they attempt something new and don't get it 'right' first time, then this could serve as proof that they lack intelligence.

Evaluative praise is closely linked to causing children to have a fixed mindset - this is because evaluative praise 'grades' children according to their perceived level of ability. For example, if we tell children that they are smart, they may feel that they have to live up to this perception of them all the time, and will start to avoid anything that may call their level of intelligence into question, for fear of disappointing us. As a result, they may start to develop an aversion to tests and exams, and it can lead to them disliking, and therefore avoiding, education and learning in the long-term.

As explained, a mindset is a set of personal beliefs and is a way of thinking that influences our behavior and attitude toward ourselves and others. However, whilst it's important to be aware of the differences between a growth mindset and a fixed mindset, it's equally important to avoid categorizing children as possessing either one or the other. We have to remember that people rarely fit neatly into one category; we all display certain characteristics of each mindset depending on our mood and the situation.

## The evolution of Mindset in children

What is quite surprising is how the mindset of children evolves according to their age. Research shows that in Kindergarten, 100% of children have a growth mindset, but this decreases to 58% once they read Grade 3!

Here are the changes in mindset across grade levels (research from '*Mindsets in the Classroom*', by M.C. Ricci, 2013):

| Grade (US) / Year (UK) | Fixed Mindset | Growth Mindset |
|---|---|---|
| Kindergarden / Year 1 | N/A | 100% |
| Grade 1/ Year 2 | 10% | 90% |
| Grade 2/ Year 3 | 18% | 82% |
| Grade 3/ Year 4 | 42% | 58% |

What explains this big increase in fixed mindsets in children, is that with every increase in grade, more students start to believe that their intelligence is a fixed trait. They start incorporating the notion that 'some people are smart and some people are not'. This notion becomes stronger as children start encountering more challenges and having more tests and are therefore graded according to their academic 'ability'. This explains the significant jump in children who develop a fixed mindset between Grades 2 and 3.

This shows that the earlier we work on developing a growth mindset in children, the better! Once this mindset is ingrained, it is still possible to change it, but it requires more time and effort.

## Assessing children's mindset

In order to help children develop a growth mindset it is useful to assess their current mindset, and you can achieve this by asking your child some simple questions. These are general questions that can be adapted to specific situations as some children may have a growth mindset and believe that they can influence the outcome for some activities, while they may have a completely fixed mindset when it comes to other things.

Your child's answers to the questions below will help to give you a better indication of whether he/she has a fixed or a growth mindset:

- Do you think that everyone can learn new things? Why?

- Do you think that some kids are born smarter than others? Why?

- Do you think that we can actually change how smart we are? Why?

Most children are likely to agree with the first question, and answer that all of us can learn. However, this is not enough to define a growth mindset as it is their answers to the following questions that will help you determine whether your child believes that their intelligence is fixed or whether they can improve it, the latter being the basis of the growth mindset.

If your child seems to display a fixed mindset, you should try implementing some of the recommendations in this book and reassess your child with similar questions after a month or so. Their mindset will have hopefully changed by then and they will be convinced that they can increase their 'cleverness' and achieve many things if they put enough effort and practice into them.

## Mistakes as opportunities for learning

*"You are not a failure until you start blaming others*
*for your mistakes"*
**John Wooden**

The other primary cause of children developing a fixed mindset is a child's interpretation of, and their attitude towards, the mistakes that they make. Making mistakes is a part of being human, so if our children are afraid of making them, they will be less likely to take on new challenges and will be very resistant to doing anything that is unfamiliar, which is hardly a good preparation for the realities of adult life.

As Carol Dweck explains, "Many parents react to their children's mistakes as though they are problematic or harmful, rather than helpful. In these cases, their children develop more of a fixed mindset". It's important to recognize that our attitude as parents has a significant influence as to whether our children are able to learn from their mistakes or become afraid of making them. Of course, it's only natural that as parents, we want to protect our children from getting hurt, feeling discouraged, or making mistakes of any kind. We love them so much that we can't bear to see them suffer, so we frequently find ourselves swooping in and 'rescuing' them from challenging situations.

Whilst we may have the best of intentions, when we intervene too much in their activities, we often rob our children of the opportunity to learn the invaluable lessons that making mistakes and the process of trial and error has to teach.

"It's particularly important for young children to have the chance to play and take risks without feeling that their parents will criticize or correct them for doing something wrong."[9]

Also, if we constantly issue our children with warnings of all the bad things that may happen, we can make them anxious about life's dangers. We inadvertently disempower them by showing them that we are not prepared to trust them and have no faith in their ability to cope with/learn from making mistakes. Phrases such as "I told you so", only serve to distance them further away from taking responsibility for their mistake and/or learning from its natural consequences, and makes children less inclined to listen to what we have to say.

Every childhood experience, if handled well, can become an invaluable learning experience. Allowing your children to make mistakes and experience their natural consequences teaches them that it's ok to get things wrong from time to time, and as a result they will become better equipped, not only at handling their mistakes, but also at preventing them in the long-term.

By demonstrating through our actions as well as our words, that it is ok to make mistakes, we are helping our children to develop a growth mindset. While if we punish, chastise or express disappointment when our children make a mistake, they are far more likely to adopt a fixed mindset, which as we have already discovered, can negatively impact upon their attitude to learning and their ability to develop new skills.

As a parent, it's important to have faith in your children that they can survive upset and disappointment because they will become more confident and resilient in the process. So for example, when trying to get them invited to a birthday party they weren't included in, or pressuring the soccer coach to give them more game time - we're not doing them any favors as we're removing valuable opportunities for our kids to develop their ★ 'disappointment' muscle. Kids need to know that it's ok to fail, and that it's normal to feel sad, anxious, or angry. They learn to succeed by overcoming obstacles, not by having us remove them.

So what we should try to do instead, however hard it may be, is start learning to identify which mistakes we need to allow our children to make. Such mistakes are known as 'affordable' mistakes (as opposed to 'unaffordable' mistakes that could result in serious upset or injury), and by allowing our children to deal with the 'natural', i.e. the immediate and logical consequences of their mistakes, means that they become much better at recovering from the upset of mistakes and finding ways to solve them in the long-term.

To summarize, it's clear that our attitude as parents has a significant influence as to whether our children learn from their mistakes or become afraid of making them and ultimately on their overall mindset. So show your children that it is important to embrace mistakes by modeling this behavior when you make one. And resist the urge to swoop in and try to rescue them from frustration and disappointment, and instead allow them the opportunity to train their 'disappointment muscles'.

# CHAPTER 3

# 10 Ways to Foster Self-Esteem and Help Your Child Develop a Growth Mindset

*"Our studies show that teaching people to have a growth mindset, which encourages a focus on effort rather than on intelligence or talent, helps make them into high achievers in school and in life."*
**Carol S. Dweck**

## Developing a growth mindset in children

What Dweck's and other neuroscientific research shows is that the brain is like a muscle - it gets stronger with use. When we communicate this same message to our children and we focus our praise on things that they can control, the effect on their attitude and ability to learn is astonishing. Helping kids to understand that the struggles we experience when we are learning new and challenging things are normal and are actually a sign of neural connections strengthening in our brains, is a powerful way to transform their attitude and their perspective. Increase of motivation, willingness to accept new challenges, and healthier reactions to failure are only a few of the benefits children experience when they understand how their brains works.[10] (See Chapter 5 for books on how to talk to kids about their brains.)

If a child has been struggling in an area of their education, by helping them to develop a growth mindset, we are empowering them to realize that if they work hard at it, then they are very likely to improve. Once children understand that their intelligence and skill levels aren't innate but rather nurtured and developed, they become naturally curious and are intrinsically motivated to problem-solve and acquire new knowledge and skills through sustained effort and hard work.

Therefore, our job as parents is to encourage our children's natural curiosity about the world around them, and allow them to make mistakes and learn through practice, repetition and the process of trial and error. In doing this, we are maximizing our child's chances of developing a lifelong love of learning and education.

The real life example of Dominic O'Brien, eight time World Memory Champion in the Introduction is a great testament to this. This realization leads children to put more hard work and effort into their studies and bolsters their love of education, meaning that they are always looking to learn more. So we need to show our children that the most important aspect of any challenge is the effort and practice they put in as this leads to them being able to achieve anything. This allows children to start focusing on improvement rather than worrying about how well they performed.

And when we stop overemphasizing our child's performance and the outcome of that performance and focus on the effort made instead, we are also helping our children to understand the intrinsic value of simply 'taking part'. This encourages them to adopt an attitude of 'effort over outcome', which means that the process of taking on new challenges becomes rewarding in itself and thus this becomes the ultimate goal.

## Being Specific and making it about them

Research has shown that the way we speak to our children, and particularly the way we praise them, has a significant impact not only on their willingness to learn and to take on challenges in life, but subsequently on their self-esteem and their behavior as a whole. This is because children naturally crave their parents' acceptance and appreciation so the way that we interact with them, including the nature of the comments that we make, directly influences the way they feel about themselves.

As we explain in Chapter 1, we therefore need to be more conscious and aware of what happens in the mind of our children after we praise them. It is important not to 'over-praise' our children with general statements such as "This is great!" or "You're so clever!" because as soon as they spot that we are so hopelessly biased that we will admire just about everything they do, our praise becomes meaningless. Our children start to doubt the sincerity of our praise, and in the long-term our words of appreciation can backfire by causing children to develop a fixed mindset. Instead of praising our children with general/evaluative words, it is more effective to acknowledge their effort, behavior or even their attitude. Praising specific aspects of their achievement in this way will help them learn to self-evaluate their abilities in the future. So, for example, Dweck's research shows that telling your child "You've done really well, you must have put a lot of effort in this", is much more effective than yet another "You've done well, you're really smart."

Often just describing something that your child has achieved, or expressing interest in the achievement by asking a question about how they did it, is the best way to praise a child. So for example saying, "I really like the way you mixed the colors in your picture", is better than, "That's a lovely picture." When we show our children that their work is interesting, it enables them to 'self-evaluate' in future rather than become dependent on our opinion or judgment.

It is also crucial to manage our expectations of what our children are able to achieve at different ages. Indeed, over-expectation can easily lead children to feel that whatever they do is never 'good enough'. Children can easily develop low self-esteem when criticized regularly, even if the criticism appears to be 'constructive'. It is important to mention what they have done well and focus on the effort they have put in (no matter what the task), before talking about how they could improve and what they could have done better (see below).

## 10 ways to foster self-esteem and help your child develop a growth mindset

### 1. Help them discover their individuality:

Self-esteem comes from feeling good about ourselves and understanding what we're good at and ultimately what makes us unique. The most effective way of achieving long-lasting change in a child's level of confidence and behavior is by increasing their internal motivation. When children engage in a behavior or activity purely for the enjoyment of it, they do so because it is intrinsically rewarding and not because they are trying to earn an external reward (see Chapter 1 for why it's important to avoid external rewards).

The first step is to help them identify their unique skills. When they are young and lack experience, it's important that we allow our children to experiment with different activities so that they can find things they enjoy and that they 'naturally' have more facility/aptitude at. This will help them enjoy the process of learning and improving, and they will be less likely to give up in the face of difficulty because they enjoy the activity.

As they grow, we can help them make a list of their skills. It's important not to make children feel that skills are innate as the idea is to make them feel that they have control over the outcomes and to not 'box them in', as it's normal for children to have more facility/aptitude at some things than others. It's good for them to recognize this and to develop these abilities, while being careful to ensure that they don't develop the feeling that they're not good at other things.

So for example, you could sit down with them and make a list of what they really enjoy and what they find easy: e.g. being good at a sport (football, gymnastics, dancing, etc.), playing a musical instrument or having some specific traits that come naturally to them. For example, they may possess traits such as being a 'helper', a 'caregiver', etc. Although this may sound like 'boxing in' or labeling children, research shows that expressing these characteristics as a trait increases the likelihood of them adopting this trait.

A great forum in which to do this is a Family Meeting (see Chapter 5). The key is to ensure that we highlight their skills in a way that doesn't sound like evaluative praise and doesn't focus on their innate character. The idea is to make children feel that they have the opportunity to develop the abilities and characteristics that make them unique.

## 2. Develop perseverance by finding things that will challenge them:

Self-esteem also comes from struggle and overcoming adversity. It's important that our children don't only do things that come easily to them and that they find (age-appropriate) challenges that they can overcome. Encouraging children to find their own solutions to problems significantly increases their confidence because it helps them to realize that they can overcome difficulties without relying on another's intervention or praise. The brain has to learn to persevere through challenges.[11]

It is therefore essential to allow children to struggle when facing challenges as this gives them the opportunity to develop perseverance, persistence and grit, which are key skills to develop an overall resilience in life.

When they encounter challenges, rather than 'saving them' by intervening, we can help them by suggesting alternatives strategies to achieve what they are trying to do. You should start by giving your child empathy for their difficulty or feeling (e.g. "You seem to have really struggled with your math homework; math can be tricky sometimes"). Then you can help them find strategies to make things less challenging, such as for example 'chunking' things, i.e. divide a bigger challenge into smaller parts to make it more achievable.

As explained in Chapter 2, up until around the age of 4 or 5, most children have a growth mindset because they find the majority of things that they do to be pretty easy. Of course, there will still be occasions when they put effort into a task or activity, but when children are very young they tend not to be aware of this. However, this doesn't mean that we shouldn't praise them for the effort that they have made. Because although they may not understand immediately, if we continue to praise them for their perseverance, over time they will begin to see that there is a direct link between how much effort they put into something and what they are able to achieve.

As children grow, they will start to encounter more challenges, some of which they will inevitably struggle with. As adults, it's easy to forget just how much you're expected to learn when you're a child, and even easier to forget the frustrations that go hand in hand with learning new skills. Best-selling author, Tim Ferriss, uses the following graph to illustrate the highs and lows of trying to acquire a new skill. His example refers to learning a new language, but the same principles can be applied to learning practically any new skill. This graph is really useful for children as it provides a visual representation of the challenges that they are likely to encounter when trying to learn something new. When children know what to expect, they can better prepare themselves for the emotions that they are likely to experience and are far less likely to become overwhelmed by them.

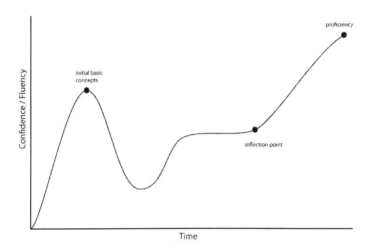

## What this chart means:

When we try our hand at a new skill or activity, generally speaking there will be an initial period of accelerated learning, which may be why so many novices appear to be blessed with 'beginner's luck'. We usually take on more information and learn quickly when we are just starting out at something and this tends to make us feel more confident, and this is no less true for children.

Once the learner has grasped the basics of a new sport, language or skill, learning starts to become more challenging because the beginner is expected to move beyond the basics and towards the more complex aspects of their chosen subject or activity. It is usually at this point that the person realizes that they aren't progressing as quickly as they were before. This almost invariably dents their confidence and negatively impacts upon their motivation to want to continue learning because their belief in themselves has decreased. It is at this point that many children (and adults!) decide to give up what they had set out to learn because it becomes 'too difficult'.

If the person perseveres in spite of this, the brain will start to adapt whatever it is they are learning to make it easier to process, essentially allowing the brain to do less to achieve the same outcome. Some people refer to this phenomenon as muscle memory or habit formation. If we refer to the graph, we see that it is at this point that the speed of learning hits a plateau - the person is still making an effort to learn and they may still have low morale due to the fact that they are not learning as quickly as they did in the beginning.

When people persevere, they will eventually reach what is known as the 'inflection point', and it is at this stage where something 'clicks' and learning suddenly becomes easier. This increased ease of learning enables the learner to become proficient at the task or skill in question if they continue practising.

This graph makes it easier to predict the level of confidence a person is likely to have a various stages of the learning process. It is particularly useful for children because it enables them to anticipate, and therefore prepare for, the emotions they are likely to experience and the difficulties they are likely to encounter, which makes it less likely that they will give up during their most challenging moments.

What we can do as parents, is that when children express frustration during a challenge and they say something along the lines of "I'm not good at this", remind them about this learning curve and the fact that they are not *yet* good at something. 'Yet' is a powerful word, which is the epitome of a growth mindset vs. a fixed one, as it reminds children that this is a temporary state and they can improve things with effort.

## 3. Celebrate challenges and mistakes:

To develop a growth mindset and resilience, children need to feel that it's normal and important to encounter challenges and to make mistakes as ultimately they can learn from them. One way to do this is to help them understand that FAIL can be thought of as a 'First Attempt In Learning' and that taking action and failing would yield less regret than failing to try in the first place.

If we feel that there is room for improvement in something they have done, instead of directly giving them 'constructive criticism', try asking them: "Are you happy with the result" (as this allows our children to tell us what they would like to improve) or "What could you do better next time?". This will give them an opportunity to self-evaluate and to be more empowered and responsible for the solutions that they decide to implement to improve things.

In this area, 'modeling' is also key (see point 10 below). For example, a good way to help children assimilate the importance of mistakes is to regularly share our mistakes or struggles and what we learned from them. A good way of doing this is to make it a part of mealtimes or include it as part of a Family Meeting (see Chapter 5), and use this time to ask our child(ren) to share their mistakes and what they have learned from them.

## 4. Praise the effort, the persistence and the progress:

It's important that we praise our children only for the traits that they have the power to change. When we focus on a child's effort and progress, rather than their achievements or level of ability, we encourage them to learn the art of motivation as we help them to recognize that sometimes tasks require us to put in effort over a long period of time. We want them to think "Yes, I worked really hard to get this result so it's worth making the effort in the future". Encouraging them to adopt this attitude will also make them less afraid of making mistakes as they start to recognize that they are an essential part of the learning process.

So rather than praising our children for getting a high grade or winning at a game or sports match, it's much more effective to praise them for the effort they have put in:

- For example, "I can see by your playing the piano how much you have practiced".

- Or "You know your times tables by heart, I can see that you have put a lot of effort into learn this".

- Or alternatively, we can ask them to explain the reason for their success - as it will usually be the effort/practice that they've put into it e.g. "Why do you think you were able to achieve such a good score on your spelling test?"

## 5. Praise descriptively and describe the 'process':

As explained in Chapter 1, it is easy to fall into the 'over-praise' trap and this actually often depends on our culture or the way we were raised. If you tend to praise your children a lot, it's important not to feel guilty about it and totally rein in your natural tendencies. Instead you can improve the way you praise by praising descriptively and describing the process (as opposed to evaluatively as explained in Chapter 1).

Focus on strategy and the process of learning rather than the outcome, and praise the steps a child takes as this shows them that each step is a necessary part of achieving something. Our child(ren) will appreciate that we have taken an interest in their work and how it was executed, and is more likely to realize their achievements and want to share them with us.

- For example, instead of saying "Wow, this picture that you've drawn is so beautiful!" try asking them a question, "How did you do this part?".

- Or describe what we see, "Wow the chicken in your drawing looks so lifelike!".

- Instead of "I'm so proud of you for getting a good grade in your exam!" try, "You must be so proud of yourself for all the effort you put into revising for your exam".

- Avoid statements such as "That picture is amazing - you're going to be the next Picasso!", and replace with "The picture you've drawn is so lifelike - it must have taken you a lot of time to add in all that detail".

## 6. Aways be honest and praise specific actions rather than their overall behavior:

Praise everything our children do and they will either discount what we are saying, or become dependent on praise for self-affirmation. Avoid praising children if they do something that they're supposed to do. For example, when they carry something to the table or throw their shirt into the hamper, a simple "Thank you" is sufficient. Even young kids can see right through false praise, so it is important to remain honest. That said, some people have a tendency to 'under-praise' in fear that doing the opposite might 'spoil' their child. Be aware that this is not good either, as children do need our encouragement and positive comments to feel good about what they do.

When we do praise our children, it's important to focus on a child's specific actions rather than their overall behavior, as this enables children to realize that their behavior is something that they choose rather than something they are and once they start to understand that they have control over how they behave, this empowers them to be able to make better choices in future.

- For example, instead of saying, "You behaved really well when Granny was here", we can say, "I really appreciated that you helped Granny get in and out of her chair during her visit."

- Or, rather than "You were so good at the grocery store today", try "Thank you for carrying the shopping basket at the grocery store today, it was really helpful".

- Instead of "You were really well-behaved at the dinner table tonight, you're such a good boy", try "Your table manners at dinner today were excellent - I really appreciate the effort you made because it makes dinnertime so much more enjoyable for everyone".

- Avoid statements such as "I'm so proud of you for being such a good boy at swimming class today", and replace with "You must be so proud of yourself for the effort you made at swim class today. I could see that you were really concentrating on every word the teacher was saying".

Also, 'staged' eavesdropping - for example praising children to a partner or another adult within their hearing - can also be a great way to acknowledge a child's specific actions.

- For example, you could say "Have you noticed how helpful Kirstie has been recently? Her room is always tidy and I never have to ask her to do her chores, she just goes ahead and does them. I love that she's maturing into such a kind and responsible girl".

- Or, "Did I tell you how well Peter is doing in English? He's been putting so much time and effort into his homework recently and the teacher said that he's been making some excellent contributions in class - and he's even reading for fun in his spare time! It's great to see that he's enjoying it so much".

## 7. Make it about them:

One of the keys to self-esteem is to have a realistic view of ourselves and self-evaluation is crucial in achieving this. What we ultimately want is for our children to develop their own power of self-evaluation and self-awareness. Without a healthy level of self-awareness, children can become 'praise junkies' who are dependent on us to tell them if they are doing well. They can develop a kind of 'false self', which they adopt and adapt to please the adults around them or to get what they need from the world. Therefore our aim as parents is to nurture a child's ability to self-evaluate and help them acknowledge their achievements.

So when our children do something that makes us feel proud, it's only natural for us to want to tell them so and we may express this by saying, "I'm so proud of you". We might think that we are doing the 'right' thing by praising them for their achievements, but this innocuous sentence makes it 'about us' rather than them without even realizing it. When we tell our children how proud we are of them, rather than boosting their self-esteem and confidence, it can actually have a much less desirable effect, in that it can make children feel pressured to live up to our high expectations. And then suddenly every achievement they make becomes about keeping us happy rather than taking part in a task or activity because they are intrinsically motivated to do so.

So here are some examples that will help you to develop their self-evaluation skills:

Instead of saying "I'm so proud of you", try asking them instead, "You have worked hard and did well on this test, are you proud of yourself?". And once they answer, "Yes I am", you can always add: "I am proud of you too!".

Instead of "You haven't studied enough for this test, which is why you had a mediocre grade", try "Are you happy with this result?". Most children are actually more demanding of themselves than we'd expect (particularly when you apply the techniques in this book!), so they will usually answer: "No, I'm not happy with this, I could've done better". And you can encourage them to find strategies/solutions that would work for them by asking "So what can you do to improve this, next time?". This will empower them to apply the strategies that they come up with, which could simply be "studying more"!

## 8. Allow your child to make choices:

When we order people to do things, we are making an assumption that they are incapable of making the decision for themselves, so it's not surprising that their reaction is usually negative because we are sending them the message that we don't 'trust' them. This also applies to children and even though they don't seem to be responsible enough to make many choices, there are actually much better alternatives to ordering them around that will boost their confidence and self-esteem.

Even kids as young as two are able to consider the consequences of their decisions. Every decision we make in life is a choice, and it is therefore essential to allow children to make decisions early on so that they are able to learn from these choices. When kids make their own (age-appropriate) choices, they feel more in control over their lives and more confident, and our role as parents is therefore to teach our children to make choices from as early an age as possible.

However, open choices can create anxiety and delay decision-making, so the best replacement for orders/commands is to offer children Limited Choices (see tool Limited Choices in Chapter 5). By offering children limited choices (that suit us!), we can empower them to think for themselves and give them a sense of autonomy, which means that they also become more responsible for their actions.

- For example, rather than "Put on your coat, we're leaving now", try "Would you like to put your coat now or once you're outside?".

- Instead of "Go and brush your teeth, it's nearly bedtime", try "Would you like to brush your teeth now, or in five minutes?"

These seemingly unimportant choices make all the difference to your children and make them much more cooperative and boosts their self-confidence. As children grow, you can start giving them more complex choices, but it's still important to also offer some simple choices. Even offering simple choices makes a huge difference when we incorporate this into our daily lives because it significantly reduces the number of orders and commands that we have to give our children.

## 9. Accentuate the positive and focus on the strategy:

It's important that we try to ensure that our positives outweigh the negatives so that we fill our children's 'I'm capable' account instead of filling the 'I'm a failure' account. To do so, focus on their uniqueness rather than on their weaknesses. There is research that estimates that children need at least three times more positive comments than negative ones to be motivated and confident.

To achieve this, reduce criticism and start by always identifying the good things in something that your child has done (be it a test, homework, a drawing, etc.), before speaking about the potential improvements. To help them understand the strategies that have worked for them (i.e. things that they can control!), ask them to explain the reason for their success and the steps they took along the way. These will usually involve practice and effort, but it can also be a different way of learning something, or the help that they have sought from someone, or who they did something with, etc.

If you feel that there is room for improvement, allow them to self-evaluate (see above), so you can simply add: "Are you happy with the result" or "What could you do better next time?". And if you have a tendency to say "No, that's not the way to do this", you can instead suggest "I see that you've done it this way. There's another way of doing it that you might prefer, shall I show it to you?".

You should ideally make the conversation about what could be improved separate from the conversation on the positives (if at all possible), as otherwise - and particularly if you often do this, your child will hear 'It's good, BUT it's not good enough'. This mindset can stay with them for the rest of their lives, and it explains why many adults suffer from the 'I'm not good enough' syndrome.

Finally, when a child's predictions or comments are overly negative, our role is not to counter their gloom with false predictions or unreasonable expectations (see tool Empathy and Validation in Chapter 5), but to teach them not to undermine their confidence with self-defeating and fixed mindset talk. So instead of offering basic reassurances to 'look on the bright side', encourage them to think about specific ways to improve a situation and bring them closer to their goals.

## 10. Lead by example:

For children to develop a growth mindset, the whole household should ideally be setting the right example as children typically imitate their parents and their mindset. So it's important that we demonstrate our growth mindset to our children as often as possible, and try to catch ourselves when we are not modeling the best example. Ideally, we should find as many opportunities as possible to demonstrate a positive attitude, and show our children that even during tough times we're always going to strive to adopt the 'glass half full' perspective. By adopting this attitude, we are demonstrating to our children that there are positives to be found in any mistake or challenge.

If we have a tendency to use negative language "I'm not any good at this" or "This is so difficult", we should try to replace them with more growth-oriented statements:

- For example, "I'm not as good as I'd like to be at this, I need to practice more".

- Or "I haven't yet mastered this, it requires a lot of effort, but I know that it'll be worth it in the end".

- Instead of, "This is difficult, I don't know why I'm bothering!", try "This is turning out to be quite the challenge, but I know I'll get there in the end if I keep at it".

- Avoid using statements such as "This is so frustrating - I'm never going to be any good at it!", and replace with "It may be challenging right now, but I know that if I put enough time and practice into it, I'll get better soon".

And when something doesn't work out as we expected:

- Instead of, "I can't believe that I made another mistake, I'm so rubbish at this!", try "It's completely normal for me to make mistakes in the early stages, but I don't mind because I know that this is all part of the learning process".

- Avoid using statements like, "I completely messed this up" and replace with "Although I didn't get it right this time, I really learned a lot from the process and I can't wait to give it another go".

# CHAPTER 4

# Real Life Examples:
# How to Develop a Growth Mindset

The stories below are real life examples taken from our own experiences and from other parents who have been coached by Best of Parenting. These stories are great illustrations of how children can develop a growth mindset at any age and in the process, improve their confidence and self-esteem.

## Real life example 1 - What to do when children encounter challenges

The following scenario is one that most parents experience with their children at some point or another. As parents, we want our children to be as active and constructive with their time as possible, so we try to schedule in many activities for them - and sometimes too many. The problem is that in our desire for our children to learn new things, acquire new skills and be productive with their time, we can actually cause them to develop a dislike of or in many cases, even a fear of learning.

The graph in Chapter 3 is a great way of illustrating this point as it shows us that it's totally natural for children to find some stages of the learning process more difficult than others. Our job as parents is to try to let our children know that it's ok to find things difficult sometimes and that it's totally natural to hit a plateau when trying to learn a new skill. It's important to remember that how we react to our children's challenging moments will have a huge impact on their attitude towards learning, and will play a major role in determining whether they are willing to try new things and whether they give up in the face of challenge and difficulty.

### Real life scenarios

Kirstie (8) is having a conversation with her parents about her ballet lessons. The parts between brackets and in italics are what Kirstie is thinking as she listens to her parents:

### Scenario A: *What not to do*

"I don't want to do ballet anymore, it's boring." Kirstie tells her parents.

"But Kirstie, you used to enjoy ballet so much?! This is surely just a phase and you'll probably love it again next time you go?"

(*As usual, you don't hear me and you're just trying to make me change my mind. Can you not see that I am really struggling with my ballet classes at the moment? It's become so hard and I'll never be any good at it!*)

Kirstie answers: "Nothing, I just don't want to do it anymore."

Her parents look at her, somewhat surprised by this admission and ask "But what about your ballet show, don't you want to show everyone how good you are?"

(*Why are they saying this to me when it clearly isn't true?*)

"And how will you ever get to be a ballerina if you don't go to class?"

"But I'm not any good at ballet, I'm nowhere near as good as the other girls, and I don't want everyone to laugh at me if I get it wrong. Ballet class is much too hard, so I've decided that I don't want to be a ballerina anymore", she replies and crosses her arms over her chest.

Her parents immediately swoop in with reassurances:

"You're such a natural when it comes to dance though Kirstie, you'd be wasting so much talent if you gave them up!"

Kirstie frowns in disbelief at her parents' words of encouragement.

(*So I'm supposed to have been born with a talent to dance? How am I supposed to believe them if they just keep telling me how brilliant I am at everything?! I don't actually believe that I have any talent at all as it's proving to be so hard, so I may as well just give up now.*)

Kirstie leaves the room and leaves her parents disappointed at not having been able to change her mind, as they really wanted her to continue ballet as they thought that they were important for her progress and development.

### Scenario B: *How to effectively deal with these types of situation*

"I don't want to do ballet anymore, it's boring." Kirstie tells her parents.

"You're now finding ballet boring?"

"Yes, it's boring and it's hard."

"You're finding it hard? We're guessing that all the stress around the ballet show and how much practice you have to put into this probably hasn't helped?"

*('How did they guess that I am freaking out at the idea of the show?')*

"Yeah… I'm not sure I'm any good at ballet as I'm finding it really hard."

"It sounds like you're finding it hard, but as you know, in this family we don't give up just because something is too hard - so what could *you* do about this?"

"I dunno", Kirstie shrugs.

"What if we told you that the way you are feeling is completely normal?"

"What do you mean?"

"Well, when we start a new activity we all go through what's called a learning curve. At first the activity seems really easy, and we tend to get really good really quickly, which makes us feel good about ourselves. But after a little bit of time, we hit a bit of a wall and start to feel that we're not learning as quickly anymore."

"And what happens then?" Kirstie asks.

"Well, then we have two choices, we can either give up or we can choose to stick at it. If we give up, then we'll be less likely to want to try new activities in future because we'll just figure that unless we have a natural talent at it, then it'll be too hard so what's the use in trying.

But if we accept that making mistakes and not getting things right first time is all part of the learning process, then we'll soon discover that with time, effort and practice, we can achieve just about anything."

"Really? So even though I'm not as good as the other girls right now, I could be if I practice hard enough?"

"Exactly! The best ballet dancers didn't get there overnight, and they don't become accomplished because they were born with a natural talent. They probably spend more time practicing each week then you spend going to school!" They got to be as good as they are because they knew that if they set their mind to it, and put in enough effort and practice, they could achieve pretty much anything they wanted to."

"Wow!", Kirstie exclaims and before her parents can say another word, she runs off to her bedroom. Seconds later she comes back downstairs with her ballet shoes on and a huge grin on her face: "Can I practice my ballet before dinner please? I want to make sure that I'm prepared for ballet class on Thursday".

"Of course you can! I guess that means that you want to continue with ballet after all then?"

"I sure do! How else am I going to be a ballerina when I'm older if I don't go to class?", she responds and skips happily away to practice her moves.

### Scenario analysis:

In the first scenario (A), Kirstie felt dismissed by her parents, and then felt that they were trying to reassure her without really paying attention to how she felt or what she had to say. And they focused on innate talent, which is something that she has no control over.

In scenario B, the key is that her parents didn't give her an opportunity to start any 'negative self-talk', as they first focused on connecting with her by using empathy (see tool in Chapter 5). This meant that Kirstie felt listened to.

They then asked Kirstie what *she* could do about the way that she was feeling, so they made her realize that this was her problem and not theirs, but clarified that in their family, people don't quit just because something is hard. They then offered her suggestions, rather than swooping in with reassurances. The explanations and solutions they offered gave Kirstie a growth mindset perspective on her difficulties, and this is the mindset that really helps children make sense of things.

Although this scenario may sound idealistic, it often happens this way if we allow our child to express their feelings, let go of the negative feelings and then help them replace these negative emotions with growth mindset strategies. If Kirstie had still reacted negatively and left the room saying that she wanted to stop ballet, the empathy displayed by the parents and the growth mindset perspective would give them the opportunity to revisit this conversation with Kirstie later on, where they could offer her other suggestions to ensure that she continues trying. And if this approach doesn't work, and as long as the parents have tried growth mindset strategies, then they may have to accept that their child might want to focus on another activity.

## Real life example 2 - Encouraging self-evaluation and highlighting the parallel between effort and skill

When our daughter Noor was five years old, we discovered all the amazing research described in this book and we learned the importance of encouraging our children to self-evaluate. This meant that we no longer just focused on our own feelings about our children, but instead we made a conscious effort to start allowing our children to express their feelings towards us and what was happening to them. So we started changing our language and instead of saying "I'm so proud of you", we replaced it with "You've been putting in so much practice and effort, you must be really proud of yourself". Our daughter's response to this was invariably: "Not really, it was easy", whatever the activity.

Six months into trying this, we were starting to really wonder if this was working with our daughter and we started doubting the effect this new language was having. But shortly after that, she came home one day from ballet and exclaimed "I am so proud of myself because I was named ballerina of the week!". We didn't immediately answer (which would've done in the past!), but instead looked at her with an approving smile and this gave her time to add: "And it's all because I've been practising really hard!". This was exactly what we had hoped for all along - not only did she feel proud of herself, which clearly improved her self-esteem and confidence, but she also understood that all the effort and hard work she had put in had enabled her to achieve this.

A few weeks later, we took Noor to see 'Cirque du Soleil' for the first time, and she was mesmerized by the circus performers. About ten minutes into the show, she turned to us and said "Wow, they must have put in so much practice to be able to do that?!". We were so pleased that she had reached this conclusion by herself; she was demonstrating that she perfectly understood what it meant to have a growth mindset and could see for herself how much practice is required to excel at something. And this important learning moment is likely to continue having a positive influence over her life for many years to come. As for us, we couldn't have been any more proud of her, although we did of course choose our words carefully when informing Noor of this fact!

## Real life example 3 - How to turn setbacks into an opportunity to increase self-esteem and help develop a growth mindset

Lots of children go through phases where they seem to dislike or start struggling with one of their subjects at school or an activity. This is a very common problem and one that many parents find themselves worrying about. The difficulty is knowing whether or not we should try to intervene, and particularly how we can improve things.

We found ourselves in this situation with our daughter, Noor, when she turned seven. Although she had incorporated a growth mindset with regards to sports such as ballet, gymnastics, swimming and tennis and some academic subjects such as math, it took us some time to realize that she had developed a fixed mindset with regards to reading and writing. She had been struggling with her reading over the last school year, and slowly but surely started to fall behind. We knew that she was struggling, but didn't worry about it too much as we recognized that all children develop at different rates, and we trusted in the education system to support her and encourage her in the areas in which she was having difficulty. We also recognized that there are countries where they delay reading until a later age, so perhaps she simply wasn't 'ready'.

We also felt that if we swooped in and tried to fix the problem, we'd blow the situation out of all proportion and probably make Noor dislike reading even more. The last thing we wanted was for her to carry her dislike of reading into adulthood. We were stuck in quite a tricky situation, feeling unsure as to what was the right thing to do. The problem was that her reluctance to read was getting worse. Not only was she struggling with the basics, but she also became really anxious when doing it and even when talking about it, especially when sitting down to read with me (Nadim).

Neither of us could really understand what was making her so anxious and over the next few months, despite our best efforts to encourage her, the problem snowballed until it actually prevented her from getting into the school we had wanted. This was our 'wake-up call', as it was clear by now that the problem wasn't going to rectify itself and it wasn't just a phase that Noor was going through. In fact, it was getting worse so now was the time for us to act.

We sat down and talked about how we had dealt with the situation thus far, and we soon realized that we hadn't allowed Noor to develop a growth mindset about reading. Although we'd encouraged her to practice her reading and made time to read with her, Carole hadn't really been consistent enough for Noor to make some steady progress, which is essential in her feeling more confident and developing more competence.

We also thought about what could be making Noor so anxious when reading with me, and realized that up to now, my impatience for her to improve had made poor Noor afraid to read with me in case she made mistakes. In order for Noor to feel more comfortable reading with me, I first had to make her feel better about herself and make her feel that mistakes are ok. I had to lower my expectations and make an effort to be more patient and empathetic with her struggle.

We decided that the best way to approach the situation was to sit down with Noor and involve her in the process of creating a reading program that we would implement over the summer holidays. Involving her in this way was a great way of encouraging her to open up and share some of the problems she had been experiencing. Plus, we knew that if she had a say in creating the schedule, she'd be far more likely to stick to it.

By taking the time to listen to Noor and showing more empathy for her struggle, we soon discovered that she was feeling frustrated at the fact that she wasn't able to keep up with kids her own age. We also learned that her teacher had made her afraid of reading and making mistakes because she had sometimes shown some frustration at Noor's slow pace (as I/Nadim had also done at home).

So over the summer holidays, we implemented this strategy. It didn't all go smoothly – there were quite a few power struggles along the way! However, with me making a conscious effort to be more patient, empathetic and flexible, and Carole striving to be more consistent in encouraging Noor to practice, we were determined that we were going to solve the problem together as a family.

With our help and encouragement, which focused on the effort and progress she was making, Noor soon realized that the more she practiced her reading, the better she got. This growth mindset didn't happen overnight, it took sustained effort, but the results couldn't have been any better.

After a couple of months of regular practice, we sat down the Sunday before starting school for a family meeting and - as we do at the beginning of each of these meetings - we shared gratitude and compliments with one another. Noor amazed us by coming up with a new initiative – she asked "Can I be grateful for myself?" "Do you mean that you want to share something that you're proud of?" we asked. "Yes! I am proud that I have finished 'Charlie and the Chocolate Factory' and that I am reading much better now, and I am enjoying it more!" she nodded excitedly. Carole and I were absolutely beaming! We thought that her idea of sharing what she is proud of during a family meeting was great and we now implement this - we ask each and every member of the family what has made them feel proud every week.

What made this situation even more valuable is that we discovered after this episode that Noor actually had a problem with her eyes that prevented her from reading 'normally'! We had seen optometrists to check her eyes in the past as we wondered if her difficulty in reading might have been due to this. She had passed all tests successfully, but this was a condition that could only be identified by specialized optometrists (Orthoptists and Behavioral Optometrists) and research led us to go see a new eye specialist. As a result, Noor began doing daily exercises to correct this eye problem and started wearing glasses to read, which made her progress much faster.

After three months of eye exercises, where Noor made only very slow progress in her reading, and which therefore required a lot of the techniques described in this book, there was a sudden acceleration of her reading pace. She now has a 'normal' reading speed for her age, so the persistence and effort were well worth it!

## What we can learn from these real life examples

As parents, our focus should be on building a growth mindset in our children, and this cannot be developed by us simply having high expectations of them. By showing them that their struggles and mistakes are completely 'normal' and being truly accepting of them, while at the same time praising their effort, progress and persistence, we can encourage them to take on new challenges and make them unafraid to make mistakes.

# CHAPTER 5

# Tools and Activities to do with Children to Develop their Self-Esteem

## Top Tools to develop self-esteem

At Best of Parenting, we have created a series of step-by-step tools to help fulfill your child's essential needs and raise their self-esteem, so that they become happier, more cooperative and more responsible. The following is a selection of these tools that are specifically designed to help nurture your child's self-esteem and maximize their chances of developing a growth mindset and a higher level of emotional intelligence.

## Tool 1: Limited Choices

Offering your children Limited Choices enables them to make decisions from a young age and helps to develop their confidence. Although these choices are generally limited to two, this autonomy gives them the opportunity to express their individual identity and values, which in turn will help to reduce power struggles and conflict and make them more willing to comply with your requests.

Limited Choices works so effectively because it allows you to share control on your terms instead of letting your child take over. It shows them that you are prepared to trust them, helps to give them a sense of control over the situation and shows them that their opinion matters and that their feelings are being heard. Offering choices also allow children to practice making decisions (good and bad) early on, so it's the best preparation for the 'real world'.

### How to give Limited Choices:

1. Think of two limited choices or options that suit you.

2. Present these choices before your child has a chance to oppose what you might suggest (i.e. before a power struggle occurs). This is why you should give Limited Choices as much as possible throughout the day by trying to replace as many order/commands as you can with a Limited Choice (or other alternative tools such as Asking Questions or Positive & Enforceable Statements).

3. Ask your child to choose between your two options. For example:

a) "Would you like to brush your teeth now or in ten minutes?"

b) "Would you rather do your homework now or after you've finished dinner?"

c) "Do you prefer the blue shirt or the red shirt?"

## Tool 2: Positive Redirection

As parents, we don't always realize how much of our interaction with our children is in the form of negative statements such as "No you can't have ice cream before dinner", or "Stop slamming that door!". In fact, research shows that 80% of parents' interaction with their children is usually negative. Of course, we have to tell our children 'No' from time to time, but the problem is that if we say it too often, it starts to lose its effectiveness over time and it can negatively affect their self-esteem and confidence in taking on challenges. Psychologists have found that by simply reducing your use of the word 'No' and other negative statements and replacing them with more positive alternatives, you can make a significant difference to your child's behavior and motivation.

## How to use Positive Redirection:

A. **If your child is asking for something that you're not willing to give them:**

1. Begin your answer with a 'Yes' regardless of whether you intend to grant the request or not. This allows you to redirect their request. For example:

   - As an answer to: "Can I have an ice cream?", try "Yes sure, you can have an ice cream after dinner" - instead of: "No, you can't have an ice cream, dinner is in half an hour".

   - As an answer to "I want this toy", use "Yes, you can put this on your birthday list" - rather than: "There's no way I'm buying you this now!".

B. **If your child is doing something that you want them to stop doing:**

1. Use a positive command (also called a 'start command') expressed firmly and try to do this without raising your voice (see example below).

2. If possible, suggest an alternative activity or an alternative way of doing things. For example:

   - "Please speak quietly" - instead of "Stop Yelling."

- "Gently pet the dog - instead of: "Stop hurting the dog."

## Tool 3: Empathy and Validation

Empathy and Validation are both essential in helping children learn to trust their feelings and developing emotional intelligence (EQ). Listening is the basis of empathy, and children feel validated and more understood when they feel listened to without judgment and aren't immediately given well-meaning advice. Strong emotions can be scary for a child who is experiencing them for the first time, so rather than try to deny them their feelings, it's much better to use it as an opportunity to connect with them instead. In other words, when we refrain from passing judgment and giving advice, children know that we have no agenda beyond being there for them. And when children trust their feelings, this has a positive impact upon their confidence and self-esteem, because they aren't afraid of experiencing strong emotions and trust themselves not to become overwhelmed by them.

### How to give Empathy and Validation:

1. **Connect with them:** The best way to do this is to appeal first to the right side of their brain, to help engage them into a more receptive state of mind.

To do this, use a soft tone of voice, get down to their level and if the circumstances allow, give them a hug. A hug is one of the most effective ways of redirecting a child's emotions because studies show that when we hug someone, this stimulates the brain's production of dopamine and oxytocin, which help to reduce stress and promote a feeling of happiness and relaxation.

2. **Don't deny your child his or her feelings or try to save them from it**: Don't tell your child: "It's going to be ok" or "Come on, it's not that bad!" or "Calm down".

3. **Do not immediately ask your child "Why are you crying?"**, even if you have no idea why they are in such emotional distress. Much of the time children find it hard to answer this question, and asking it of them doesn't help them process their emotion. If you really need to because your child is not sharing the reason, you can ask this after following the steps below.

4. **Meet them 'where they are' by acknowledging your child's feelings and help name their feelings:** Your child may not be able to understand, acknowledge or explain the emotion they are experiencing, therefore you can help them by

reading the signs of an emotional state in their behavior and body language (just as one might look for the tell-tale signs of tiredness). This includes 'negative' emotions such as anger or sadness. Helping them put a name on their emotions enables them to 'own' this feeling, and therefore control it. Words are not only empowering, but they also 'normalize' situations, turning them from an unknown, amorphous mass into something knowable and manageable[12]. For example:

a. When your child is upset and throwing a tantrum: "You seem really frustrated and angry", or "You seem to have a lot of trouble coping with what I just told you?"

b. When your child has hurt themselves: "Oh, this must hurt!" or "You seem in a lot of pain, the fall must have been harder than it looked?"

c. When your child is getting very angry with their sibling: "I can see that this situation is upsetting you".

**Once you've given them empathy, you can help your child redirect their emotions.**

When you children are younger, an effective way to do this is to put them in 'thinking mode'. Here are some examples:

a. When your child is upset and throwing a tantrum, you can give them a choice. For example: "Would you like to come with me to your room and play a game or stay here on the floor?"

b. When your child has hurt themselves: "Do you need help getting up or can you do it by yourself?" or "Does this hurt a lot, average or just a bit?" or "Would a hug make you feel better?"

c. In most other situations, you can ask your child: "Is there something that I can do to help?"

## Tool 4: Problem Solving

As parents, we often skip straight to offering solutions to our children when they present us with a problem, or to implementing consequences or punishment when they misbehave, without giving them the opportunity to solve their own issues or to try to understand the reasons for their behavior. In doing so, we are underestimating their ability to solve their own problems, and we are not giving them a chance to participate in finding solutions to these problems for themselves. The Problem Solving tool empowers your children to find solutions to their own problems, rather than focusing on consequences and punishment (which can have detrimental effects on motivation). It's a great way of teaching your child to think for themselves and encourages them to be responsible for their own actions, which makes it far more effective than any other form of discipline and provides a great boost to confidence and self-esteem.

**How to use Problem Solving:**

This tool can be used in two different ways:

1. **When *your child* has a problem, which they tell you about:** For example, they have no friends, they don't like an activity anymore such as Kirstie's example in Chapter 4, or they are struggling to do their homework on time (which by the way is their problem, not yours!):

   a) **Encourage your child to take ownership of their problem** by asking them, "What could YOU do about this?". The answer to this question is usually, "I don't know", particularly if they've not been 'coached' to find solutions to their own problems before.

So you can respond to this by saying, "Do you want me to help give you some ideas to start with?" or "Would you like me to tell you what some other children have tried?"

b) If they say "No thank you", say **"Ok, but if you change your mind, I'm always here to listen."**

c) If they say "Yes please", **give them some different options of possible solutions.** Offer them at least two solutions.

d) **Empower**: After you explain each solution, encourage your child to evaluate it by asking, "How would that work for you?". If you can't come up with any ideas straight away, simply say to your child, "Let me have a think about it and check how other kids have dealt with this problem and I'll get back to you".

e) **Show interest, but avoid interfering**: Once your child has decided on which solution they think would be the most appropriate course of action (either one that you have suggested or one they have come up with themselves), all you need to say is, "Let me know how it all works out - good luck!".

2. **When *you* have a problem that you want to discuss with your child:** Perhaps you would like your child to improve a certain aspect of their behavior and you want to involve your child in finding solutions to this issue:

   a) **Initiate a problem-solving session:** The most effective way of doing this is by doing something that your child enjoys or alternatively, you can incorporate this session into a family meeting. Identify exactly what the issue is without blaming your child for the behavior, while explaining why this doesn't work for you.

   b) **Ask your child questions that show that you're in it together:** "What could WE do about this?"

   c) **Work together with your child to generate what possible solutions there may be to the problem in question.** Talk about what you could both do differently next time the problem presents itself.

   d) **Listen to their suggestions carefully,** asking them: "And how do you think that would work for you?"

e) **Have a brainstorming session:** Decide on what you each think are the best solutions and then brainstorm together about how you could implement them.

f) **Ask your child how they would prefer to be reminded should they break your agreement:** If they don't have any ideas of their own, help them come up with a fun way to remind them.

## Tool 5: Family meetings

Holding regular family meetings is key to building and maintaining a strong connection with your children and to building their confidence and self-esteem. It provides the perfect forum in which to give encouragement and praise and to discuss challenges and how to overcome them.

It's also a way of making sure that all family members feel a sense of belonging and responsibility towards one another, and it provides an invaluable opportunity for each person to have their thoughts heard and their feelings acknowledged. This in itself is incredibly powerful as it helps to create a feeling of family unity and togetherness and a stronger sense of confidence in the strength of the family bond.

## How to hold Family Meetings:

1. Schedule in (ideally) one family meeting every week.

2. Although it may sound quite formal, to make the meeting run more smoothly, we recommend electing two family members to act as Chair-Person and Secretary (who will be responsible for taking notes of the meeting).

3. Open the meeting with compliments and gratitudes. Each person should take a turn addressing every family member to express a gratitude or give a compliment. This is a great opportunity to use your new skills in order to praise the effort and progress that your children have made over the previous week(s). It also significantly boosts their confidence as they feel that they are noticed and acknowledged.

4. Ask every family member to share a moment that they have been proud of since the last meeting. Another great confidence booster!

5. Go through the 'Agenda', which may include one or more of the following:

- Individual issues, each family member has the opportunity to raise their need or identify a problem they may be experiencing.

- Hold a Problem Solving session to deal with any individual issues.

- Decide on a task/chore system: allocate tasks and household duties.

- Plan activities and family fun days.

- Play a game or have a sing-song.

- It may sound a bit cheesy, but it adds to the sense of bonding to end the meeting with a family hug!

## Other Activities that will help develop confidence and self-esteem:

### 1. Developing self-awareness and goals:

As explained in Chapter 2 and 3, self-awareness is a key component of self-esteem as it increases your child's ability to understand what they are good at and to be realistic about what they can achieve. Setting goals is also a great way to achieve something over a long period of time, as it helps to develop self-esteem and allows children to make mistakes that will teach valuable lessons.

Here are some ideas that can help develop their self-awareness:

- Ask your child (ideally in a Family Meeting) to share what they consider to be their greatest strength and their greatest achievement to date. Does their self-evaluation match your own opinion?

- Ask them to share one or two goals/dreams they'd like to achieve in the next 12 months. Ask them to be specific about the nature of this goal and how they will achieve it. For example, if they want to be able to play the piano in front of an audience in 12 months, or if they'd like to be part of the school's football team, what are the steps to achieving this. If they come up with negative self-talk, find ways to show them why this is a fixed mindset and how a growth mindset can help them to achieve their goal(s).

## 2. Teaching them how their brain works:

As explained in Chapter 3, this can really help foster a growth mindset as it shows children that the brain is a muscle that can be developed. It's a great way of demonstrating to them that when we practice something new, the 'neural connections' that our synapses make get stronger and the easier things get. Here are some useful books that can help you initiate a discussion with your child about how their brain works:

- For younger children: Your Fantastic Elastic Brain Stretch it, Shape it by JoAnn Deak.

- For older children: My First Book About the Brain by Patricia J. Wynne or The Owner's Manual for Driving Your Adolescent Brain by JoAnn Deak

- There are also several useful videos about what it means to have a growth mindset on Youtube. This series of 5 short videos from Class Dojo is really well done (although we do not sub-scribe to the philosophy behind their app!): https://www.youtube.com/watch?v=2zrtHt3-bBmQ

### 3. Improving memory:

As Dominic O'Brien's story demonstrates, a good memory can be a great confidence booster. You can help your children develop their memory from an early age by playing memory games with them. Here are a couple of games that will help improve their memory:

- You have most probably already heard of the game: 'I went to the market and bought'? This is a great way to develop memory because creating a story around a situation is a proven method to help people remember things. One person starts saying: "I went to the market and bought" and chooses an item. Each participant takes a turn and must recite what the others have said in the right order whilst also adding an extra item to the list.

- Another enjoyable and useful game is to place 10 items on a table and ask your child to memorize the objects for a minute or two. Then ask them to turn their back, allowing you to remove an item. They then look at the remaining objects and have a limited time (depending on their age) to guess which one you removed.

## 4. Teaching them about how to use their body to increase their confidence:

Body language can influence their confidence. If you can teach your children to show confidence through their body language, this will affect their state of mind and they will feel more confident as a result, which then becomes a self-reinforcing cycle.

Breathing is also a great way to increase confidence by reducing stress and anxiety in cases of challenging situations. Deep, mindful breathing - which means breathing from the belly - is one of the most effective ways of reducing stress and allowing us to make calm and rational decisions. Breathing for around three minutes per day from an early age (and increasing this as they grow) is important to practice with children as it helps give them a sense of control over their own emotions and reactions to things.

For more details on the tools described above and to discover more techniques that can help address all types of common parenting challenges such as lack of cooperation, whining and arguing and homework battles, you can also read '*Kids*

*Don't Come With a Manual - The Essential Guide to a Happy Family Life'*, or *'The Working Parents' Guide to Raising Happy and Confident Children'*.

# Conclusion

As we've seen, self-esteem and confidence are key to success and there are many ways in which we can help to develop these traits in our children. Being aware of the impact that our words and actions have upon our child's personal development and their sense of self is an essential part of this process. We also need to be aware of the most common parenting mistakes so we can avoid making them and prevent our children from adopting a fixed mindset.

Because although there is no such thing as a 'perfect parent', there are steps that each one of us can take to become more effective in our approach to parenting and equip our children with all the tools they need to be able to thrive. Of course, there will still be difficulties and challenges along the way, but never despair. As the real life examples shared in this book demonstrate, there are countless examples of children who appear to dislike school and other forms of learning and may be labeled as lazy and not 'capable' by their teachers and others, but who still go on to achieve great things in life.

We must remember that as parents, one of the most important jobs we have is to show our children that we will always believe in them, no matter what. When we allow our children to make affordable mistakes and they see that we have faith in their ability to survive hurt, upset and disappointment, they start to develop more faith in themselves. And when we empower our children to believe in themselves, we also empower them to become happy and independent adults. So when spending time with your children, keep the following points in mind:

- Show children how to celebrate their mistakes by embracing yours as this will help make them more resilient and will increase their willingness to take on new challenges.

- Refrain from rescuing them from difficult experiences and unpleasant emotions - this will help train their 'disappointment muscles', and better prepares them for the realities of adult life.

- Help them to see that in every difficulty or challenge they face lies an opportunity for learning and growth.

- Always focus on the effort and progress your child has made when participating in a task, exam or activity rather than the outcome as this will help them to develop a growth mindset and the art of self-motivation.

- Be selective and honest in the praise that you give and remember to ask them questions to help them self-evaluate (such as "You must be proud of yourself given all the effort you've put into this") before giving your own 'judgment' and praise.

If you are consistent in the application of the tools in this book, you can maximize the chances that your children will one day - hopefully sooner rather than later - develop a growth mindset, find their passion(s) and become completely responsible for their own success.

If you've found this book helpful and would like to equip yourself with more of our highly effective tools that are designed to suit any parenting style, you can discover this and a whole lot more in our book *'Kids Don't Come With a Manual - The Essential Guide to a Happy Family Life'*.

And if you're a busy working parent, you may prefer to read the condensed version *'The Working Parents' Guide to Raising Happy and Confident Children'*, which draws on the parallels between leadership and parenting.

# Resources and Further Reading

Aldort, Naomi, *Raising our Children, Raising Ourselves*, Book Publishers Network, 2005

Bronson, Po and Merryman, Ashley, *Nurture Shock*, Ebury Press, 2009

Biddulph, Steve, Raising Boys, Harper Thorsons, 2010

Cohen, Lawrence, Playful Parenting, Ballantine Books, 2012

Dreikurs, Rudolf, *Children: The Challenge*, First Plume Printing, 1990

Dweck, Carol, *Mindset: The New Psychology of Success*, Ballantine Books, 2007

Faber, Adele and Mazlish, Elaine, *How to Talk so Kids Will Listen and Listen so Kids Will Talk*, Avon Books, 1999

Faber, Adele and Mazlish, Elaine, *Siblings Without Rivalry*, Piccadilly Press, 1999

Fay, Jim and Cline, Foster, *Parenting with Love and Logic*, Navpress, 2006

Fay, Jim and Charles, *Love and Logic Magic for Early Childhood*, Love and Logic, 2000

Gordon, Thomas, *Parent Effectiveness Training*, Three River Press, 2000

Goleman, Daniel, *Emotional Intelligence: Why it Can Matter More Than IQ*, Bloomsbury, 1996

Gottman, John, *Raising an Emotionally Intelligent Child*, Simon and Chuster, 1997

Ginott, Haim, *Between Parent and Child*, Crown Publications, 2004

Hawn, Goldie, *10 Mindful minutes*, Piatkus, 2011

James, Oliver, *They F\*\*\* You Up: How to Survive Family Life*, Bloomsbury, 2006

James, Oliver, *How not to f\*\*\* them up*, Vermillion, 2011

Kohn, Alfie, *Unconditional Parenting*, Atria Books, 2005

Kohn, Alfie, *Punished by Rewards*, Houghton Mifflin, 2000

Markham, Laura, *Peaceful Parent, Happy Kids*, Penguin Books, 2012

Medina, John, *Brain Rules - 12 principles for surviving and thriving at work, home and school*, Pear Press, 2014

Mischel, Walter, *The Marshmallow Test: Mastering Self-control*, Little Brown and Company, 2014

Nelsen, Jane, *Positive Discipline*, Ballantine Books, 2013

Nelsen, Jane and Lott, Lynn, and Glen, Stephen, *A-Z*, Three Rivers Press, 2007

Mc Cready, Amy, *If I Have To Tell You One More Time*, Penguin, 2012

Palmer, Sue, *Toxic Childhood*, Orion Books, 2007

Palmer, Sue, *Detoxing Childhood*, Orion Books, 2008

Reivich, Karen and Shatte, Andrew, *The Resilience Factor*, Three Rivers Press, 2002

Sanders, Matthew, *Every Parent*, Penguin Books, 2004

Shefali Tsabary, *The Conscious Parent: Transforming Ourselves, Empowering Our Children*, Namaste Publishing, 2010

Siegel, Daniel, *Parenting From the Inside Out*, Jeremy P. Tarcher, 2003

Siegel, Daniel, *The Whole Brain Child*, Bantam, 2012

Stoll Lillard, Angeline, *Montessori - The science behind the genius*, Oxford University Press, 2007

Webster-Stratton, *The Incredible Years*, Incredible Years, 2005

# Endnotes

1 Burton, Neel, Psychology Today, October 2015 https://www.psychologytoday.com/blog/hide-and-seek/201510/self-confidence-versus-self-esteem

2 Olszewski-Kubilius, Talent development as an emerging framework for gifted education, 2013

3 O'Brien, Dominic, *You can have an amazing memory*, 2011, Watkins Publishing

4 Dweck, Carol, Mindset: The New Psychology of Success, Ballantine Books, 2007

5 Fay, Charles, Finding your Children's Gifts, Love and Logic

6 Henderlong and Lepper, *The Effects of Praise*, 2002

http://www.parentingscience.com/effects-of-praise.html

7 Warneken and Tomasello - *Extrinsic rewards undermine altruistic tendencies in 20-month-olds* - Dev Psychol. 2008 Nov

8   Dweck, Carol, Mindset: The New Psychology of Success, Ballantine Books, 2007

9   Kathy Hirsh-Pasek, PhD, professor of psychology at Temple University, Philadelphia

10  Ricci, Mary Cay and Lee, Margaret, *Mindset for Parents* - Prufrock Press, 2016

11  Bronson, Po and Merryman, Ashley, *Nurture Shock*, Ebury Press, 2009

12  Gottman, John, *Raising an Emotionally Intelligent Child,* 1998, Prentice Hall & IBD

Made in the USA
Charleston, SC
07 February 2017